All-in-One
Chinese Fun
Student Book

Sing, Play, and Speak Chinese

Hazel Young Hasegawa

CHENG & TSUI COMPANY

Boston

16 15 14 13 12   1 2 3 4 5 6 7 8 9 10

First edition 2013

Published by
Cheng & Tsui Company, Inc.
25 West Street
Boston, MA 02111-1213 USA
Fax (617) 426-3669
www.cheng-tsui.com
"Bringing Asia to the World"™

ISBN 978-0-88727-830-3

Printed in the United States of America

Contents

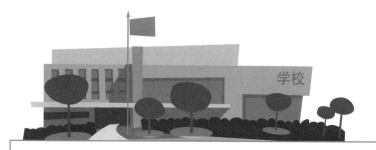

Home-School Connection

Welcome to *All-in-One Chinese Fun!* Using this program, your child will learn basic Chinese through song and play. As your child learns Chinese at school, you can share his or her language progress through this Student Book.

The Student Book includes songs in Chinese written to familiar tunes, activities, and a musical version of "Cinderella." Just as with their first language, children initially learn their first Chinese words phonetically through repetition. The song lyrics in this book will help you practice the language with your child in a fun, playful way. *Pinyin* (phonetic English pronunciations) and English translations are provided for you to understand the content of the lessons.

In the back of the book is your child's own copy of the *All-in-One Chinese Fun* CD. The first 12 tracks of the CD are recorded versions of the songs, performed in lively arrangements that you and your child can listen to and sing along with. The second half of the CD contains chanted versions of the songs, performed by native Chinese-speaking children to reinforce the Chinese words.

Have fun!

Songs

Song 1

在哪里?

Zài Nǎli?

Sung to the tune of "Where Is Thumbkin?"

手 在 哪 里? 手 在 哪 里? 在 这 里。 在 这 里。
Shǒu zài nǎ li? Shǒu zài nǎ li? Zài zhè li. Zài zhè li.

你 今 天 好 吗? 我 今 天 很 好。 谢 谢 你, 谢 谢 你。
Nǐ jīn tiān hǎo ma? Wǒ jīn tiān hěn hǎo. Xiè xie ni, xiè xie ni.

手
shǒu

头
tóu

脚
jiǎo

Where Is It?

Where is your hand? Where is your hand? Here it is. Here it is.
How are you today? Today I am very well. Thank you, thank you.

Yī Èr Sān

Sung to the tune of "This Is the Way We Wash Our Hands"

一　二　三，　一　二　三　一　二　三　四　五　六　七。
Yī　èr　sān,　yī　èr　sān,　yī　èr　sān　sì　wǔ　liù　qī.

一　二　三　四　五　六　七　八　九　十。
Yī　èr　sān　sì　wǔ　liù　qī　bā　jiǔ　shí.

One, Two, Three

One, two, three, one, two, three, one, two, three, four, five, six, seven.
One, two, three, four, five, six, seven, eight, nine, ten.

明天见
Míngtiān Jiàn

Sung to the tune of "Twinkle, Twinkle, Little Star"

1. 再 见 再 见 明 天 见。 谢 谢 老 师 明 天 见。
   Zài jiàn zài jiàn míng tiān jiàn. Xiè xie lǎo shī míng tiān jiàn.

2. 再 见 再 见 我 爱 你。 谢 谢 妈 妈 我 爱 你。
   Zài jiàn zài jiàn wǒ ài nǐ. Xiè xie mā ma wǒ ài nǐ.

老师
lǎoshī

妈妈　　　**爸爸**
māma　　　bàba

See You Tomorrow

Good-bye, good-bye. See you tomorrow. Thank you, Teacher. See you soon.
Good-bye, good-bye. I love you. Thank you, Mom. I love you.

我们大家来拍拍手

Wǒmen Dàjiā Lái Pāipāi Shǒu

我 们 大 家 来 拍 拍 手， 我 们 大 家 来 拍 拍 手。
Wǒ men dà jiā lái pāi pāi shǒu, wǒ men dà jiā lái pāi pāi shǒu.

我 们 大 家 来 拍 拍 手， 大 家 拍 拍 手。
Wǒ men dà jiā lái pāi pāi shǒu, dà jiā pāi pāi shǒu.

点点头
diǎndiǎn tóu

弯弯腰
wānwān yāo

踏踏脚
tàtà jiǎo

Let's All Clap Hands

Let's all clap hands, let's all clap hands.
Let's all clap hands, everybody clap your hands.

伊比呀呀

Yī Bǐ Yā Yā

Sung to the tune of "She'll Be Coming 'Round the Mountain"

伊 比　　　呀 呀　　伊 比 伊 比　　呀。
Yī bǐ　　　yā yā　　yī bǐ yī bǐ　　yā.

伊 比　　　呀 呀　　伊 比 伊 比　　呀。
Yī bǐ　　　yā yā　　yī bǐ yī bǐ　　yā.

伊 比　　　呀 呀　　伊 比 伊 比　　呀 呀
Yī bǐ　　　yā yā　　yī bǐ yī bǐ　　yā yā

伊 比 伊 比 呀　呀　伊 比 伊 比　呀。
yī bǐ yī bǐ yā　yā　yī bǐ yī bǐ　yā.

Yi Bi Ya Ya

This song is made up of nonsense syllables. Have fun with it!

我的朋友在哪里?

Wǒ de Péngyou Zài Nǎli?

一 二 三 四 五 六 七, 我 的 朋 友 在 哪 里?
Yī èr sān sì wǔ liù qī, wǒ de péng you zài nǎ li?

在 这 里! 在 这 里! 1. 我 的 朋 友 在 这 里!
Zài zhè li! Zài zhè li! Wǒ de péng you zài zhè li!

2. 我 的 朋 友 就 是 你!
Wǒ de péng you jiù shì nǐ!

Where Is My Friend?

One, two, three, four, five, six, seven, where is my friend?

Over here! Over here! My friend is over here!

You are my friend!

Song 7

老师早呀
Lǎoshī Zǎo Ya

老 师 早 呀!　　小 朋 友 也 早!
Lǎo shī zǎo ya!　　Xiǎo péng you yě zǎo!

我 们 今 天　大 家 都 早 呀!
Wǒ men jīn tiān　dà jiā dōu zǎo ya!

Good Morning, Teacher

Good morning, Teacher!
Good morning, Students!

Today we all say, "Good morning!"

蜗牛

Wōniú

喂　喂　　蜗　牛,　　喂 喂 蜗　牛!
Wèi　wei　　wō　niú,　　wèi wei wō　niú!

你 有 没 有　眼 睛?　你 有 没 有　头?
Nǐ yǒu méi yǒu　yǎn jing?　Nǐ yǒu méi yǒu　tóu?

我 有 眼 睛,　我 有 眼 睛,　还 有 头, 有　脚。
Wǒ yǒu yǎn jing,　wǒ yǒu yǎn jing,　hái yǒu tóu, yǒu　jiǎo.

Hey, Snail

Hey, hey, snail, hey, hey, snail.

Do you have eyes? Do you have a head?

I have eyes, I have eyes and a head and feet.

一个，两个，三个朋友

Yí ge, Liǎng ge, Sān ge Péngyou

Sung to the tune of "Michael Finnegan"

一 个，两 个，三 个 朋 友，四 个，五 个，六 个 朋 友。
Yí ge, liǎng ge, sān ge péng you, sì ge, wǔ ge, liù ge péng you.

七 个，八 个，友 个 朋 友，十 个 小 朋 友。
Qī ge, bā ge, jiǔ ge péng you, shí ge xiǎo péng you.

苹果
píngguǒ

桌子
zhuōzi

椅子
yǐzi

One, Two, Three Friends

One, two, three friends, four, five, six friends.
Seven, eight, nine friends, ten little friends.

两只老虎
Liǎng zhī Lǎohǔ

Sung to the tune of "Frère Jacques"

两 只 老 虎, 两 只 老 虎, 跑 得 快!
Liǎng zhī lǎo hǔ, liǎng zhī lǎo hǔ, pǎo de kuài!

跑 得 快! 一 只 没 有 耳 朵, 一 只 没 有 尾 巴。
Pǎo de kuài! Yì zhī méi yǒu ěr duo, yì zhī méi yǒu wěi ba.

真 奇 怪! 真 奇 怪!
Zhēn qí guài! Zhēn qí guài!

斑马
bānmǎ

狮子
shīzi

大象
dà xiàng

老虎
lǎohǔ

Two Tigers

Two tigers, two tigers,
Running fast, running fast!
One has no ears, one has no tail.
Very Strange! Very Strange!

Song 11

哈哈哈
Hā Hā Hā

哈　哈　哈　　哈　哈　哈，　大家　哈　哈　　笑！
Hā　hā　hā　　hā　hā　hā，　dà jiā　hā　hā　　xiào!

你　也　笑，　我　也　笑，　大家　哈　哈　　笑。
Nǐ　yě　xiào，　wǒ　yě　xiào，　dà jiā　hā　hā　　xiào.

哈　哈　哈　拍拍　手！　哈　哈　哈　点点　头！
Hā　hā　hā　pāi pāi shǒu!　Hā　hā　hā　diǎn diǎn tóu!

你　也　笑，　我　也　笑，　大家　哈　哈　　笑。
Nǐ　yě　xiào，　wǒ　yě　xiào，　dà jiā　hā　hā　　xiào.

跑一跑
pǎo yi pǎo

Let's Laugh

Ha, ha, ha. Ha, ha, ha, everybody, laugh, "ha ha!"
You laugh, too, I laugh, too, everybody, laugh, "ha ha!"
Ha, ha, ha, clap your hands! Ha, ha, ha, nod your head!
You laugh, too, I laugh, too, everybody, laugh, "ha ha!"

你叫什么名字?

Nǐ Jiào Shénme Míngzi?

Sung to the tune of "London Bridge Is Falling Down"

你　叫　什么名字　什么名字,什么名字?

Nǐ　jiào　shén me míng zi,　shén me míng zi, shén me míng zi?

你　叫　什么名字　我　叫　_____。

Nǐ　jiào　shén me míng zi?　Wǒ　jiào　_____.

What Is Your Name?

What is your name, your name, your name?

What is your name? I'm called _____.

Activities

Activity 1

Where Is It?

Can you help John's dog find its way home?

One, Two, Three

Roll the game cube and count out the spaces.
Climb up ladders, but slide down snakes!

Activity 3

See You Tomorrow

Draw yourself saying 你好 or 再见 to your 老师!

你好!   再见!

Let's All Clap Hands

Play Tic-Tac-Toe. When you place your game piece on a square, say the action and act it out!

拍拍手	点点头	弯弯腰
弯弯腰	拍拍手	踏踏脚
踏踏脚	点点头	拍拍手

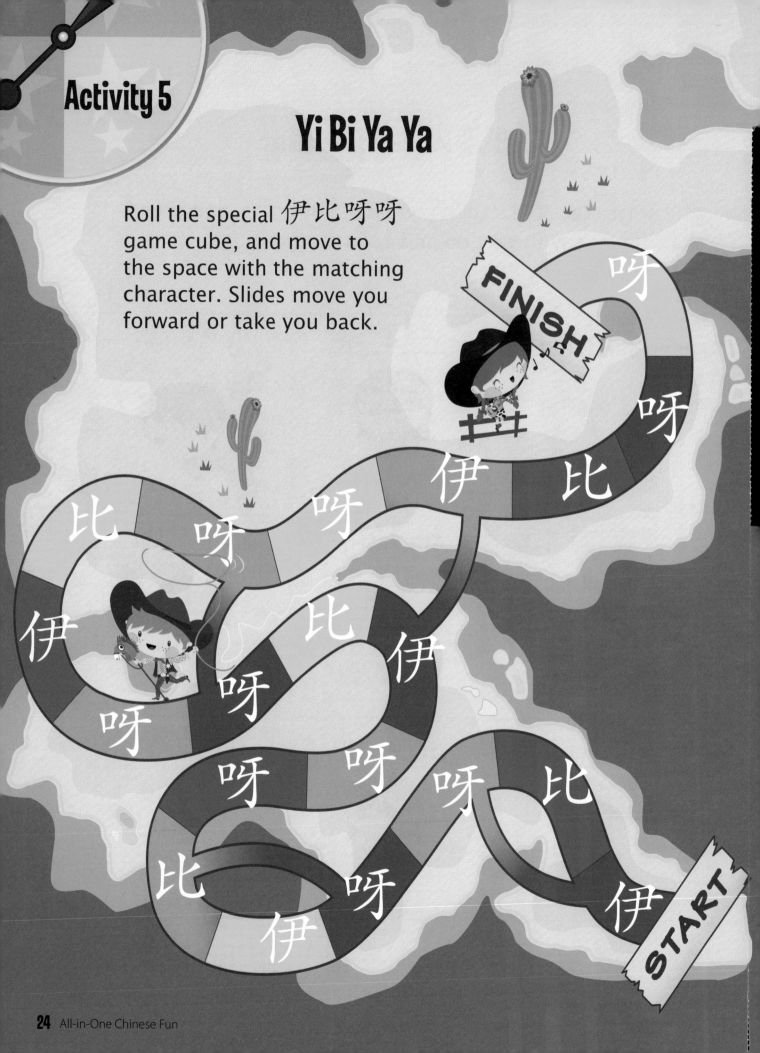

Activity 5

Yi Bi Ya Ya

Roll the special 伊比呀呀 game cube, and move to the space with the matching character. Slides move you forward or take you back.

Where Are My Friends?

Count and circle the friends in the picture.
Write the number on the line.

有 _____ 个朋友。

Activity 7

Good Morning, Teacher!

Find the puzzle piece that matches the first one in each row.

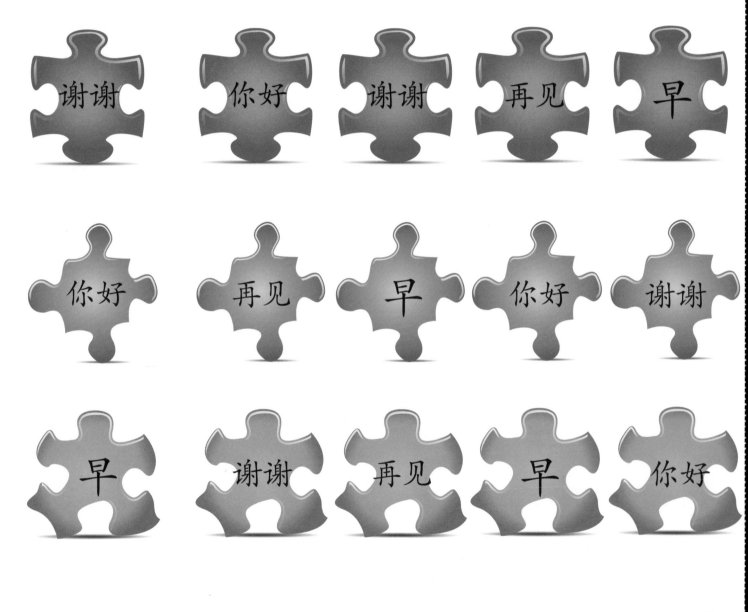

谢谢 · 你好 · 谢谢 · 再见 · 早

你好 · 再见 · 早 · 你好 · 谢谢

早 · 谢谢 · 再见 · 早 · 你好

再见 · 再见 · 你好 · 谢谢 · 早

Two Tigers

Use the body parts to draw your own tiger!

眼睛   耳朵   尾巴

Write the number on the line.

我的老虎有＿二＿个嘴巴。

我的老虎有＿＿＿个眼睛。

我的老虎有＿＿＿个脚。

我的老虎有＿＿＿个耳朵。

我的老虎有＿＿＿个尾巴。

Activity 11

Let's Laugh

Count the laughs in each row.
Then write the Chinese number on the line.

1. 哈哈哈哈哈哈 　　_____次

2. 哈哈哈 　　_____次

3. 哈哈哈哈 　　_____次

4. 哈哈哈哈哈 　　_____次

5. 哈哈哈哈哈哈哈 　　_____次

学校

What Is Your Name?

Draw a friend, your teacher, and yourself! Write the names on the lines.

我朋友叫 _____ 。

我老师叫 _____ 。

我叫 _____ 。

Drama

灰姑娘

Huīgūniáng

Cinderella

Characters		

Narrator	King's Messenger	Fairy Godmother
Cinderella	Stepsister 1	Stepsister 2
Chorus	Stepmother	Prince

Cinderella

	Scene 1

Narrator:

Hěnjiǔ hěnjiǔ yǐqián,

很 久 很 久 以 前，

Once long, long ago,

Yíge nǚháir jiào Huīgūniáng.

一 个 女 孩 儿 叫 灰 姑 娘。

There lived a girl named Cinderella.

Cinderella:

Wǒ méiyǒu bàba, māma.

我 没 有 爸 爸 、 妈 妈。

I have no father and no mother.

Měitiān yào sǎodì.

每 天 要 扫 地。

Every day I sweep the floor.

Chorus: *(Sung to the tune of the chorus of "Jingle Bells")*

扫 扫 地，　扫 扫 地，　我 要 扫 扫　　　地，

Sǎo sǎo dì,　sǎo sǎo dì,　wǒ yào sǎo sǎo　　　dì,

Sweep the floor, sweep the floor, I will sweep the floor,

扫 扫 地，　扫 扫 地，　我 要 扫 扫　　　地。

Sǎo sǎo dì,　sǎo sǎo dì,　wǒ yào sǎo sǎo　　　dì,

Sweep the floor, sweep the floor, I will sweep the floor.

灰姑娘

Cinderella:
Wǒ měitiān yào xǐwǎn.

我 每天 要 洗碗。

Every day I wash the dishes.

Chorus: *(Sung to the tune of the chorus of "Jingle Bells")*

洗 洗 碗， 洗 洗 碗， 我 要 洗 洗 碗。
Xǐ xǐ wǎn, xǐ xǐ wǎn, wǒ yào xǐ xǐ wǎn.

Wash the dishes, wash the dishes, I will wash the dishes.

洗 洗 碗， 洗 洗 碗， 我 要 洗 洗 碗。
Xǐ xǐ wǎn, xǐ xǐ wǎn, wǒ yào xǐ xǐ wǎn.

Wash the dishes, wash the dishes, I will wash the dishes.

Cinderella:
Měitiān yào zuòfàn.

每天 要 做饭。

Every day I cook the meals.

Chorus: *(Sung to the tune of the chorus of "Jingle Bells")*

做 做 饭， 做 做 饭， 我 要 做 做 饭，
Zuò zuò fàn, zuò zuò fàn, wǒ yào zuò zuò fàn,

Cook the meals, cook the meals, I will cook the meals,

做 做 饭， 做 做 饭， 我 要 做 做 饭。
Zuò zuò fàn, zuò zuò fàn, wǒ yào zuò zuò fàn.

Cook the meals, cook the meals, I will cook the meals.

Cinderella

Scene 2

King's Messenger: Qǐng zhùyì! Qǐng zhùyì!

请 注意！请 注意！

Attention! Attention!

Wángzǐ qǐng dàjiā lái tiàowǔ!

王子 请 大家 来 跳舞！

The prince invites everyone to the ball!

Stepsister 1: Wǒmen yào chuān piàoliàng de yīfu!

我们 要 穿 漂亮 的 衣服！

We will wear our beautiful clothes!

Stepsister 2: Shū piàoliàng de tóufa!

梳 漂亮 的 头发！

We will do our hair beautifully!

Narrator: Dàjiā dōu qù tiàowǔ,

大家 都 去 跳舞，

Everyone was going to go to the ball,

Kěshì Huīgūniáng bùnéng qù.

可是 灰姑娘 不能 去。

But Cinderella was not allowed to go.

Stepmother : Nǐ bùxǔ qù!

你 不许 去！

You are not allowed to go!

灰姑娘

Chorus: *(Sung to the tune of the chorus of "Jingle Bells")*

不 许 去， 不 许 去， 你 不 许 去，
Bù xǔ qù, bù xǔ qù, nǐ bù xǔ qù,
Cannot go, cannot go, you aren't allowed to go,

不 许 去， 不 许 去， 我 不 许 你 去。
Bù xǔ qù, bù xǔ qù, wǒ bù xǔ nǐ qù.
Cannot go, cannot go, I won't let you go.

Narrator :

Huīgūniáng jiù kūle.

灰 姑 娘 就 哭 了。

Cinderella cried.

Scene 3

Narrator:

A, hūrán, xiānnǚ láile.

啊，忽然 仙女 来了.

Suddenly, there appeared a fairy godmother.

Fairy Godmother:

Huīgūniáng, bié kū, wǒ lái bāng nǐ.

灰 姑 娘 ，别 哭 ，我 来 帮 你 。

Cinderella, don't cry, I will help you.

Shuā! Biàn! Shuā! Biàn!

唰! 变! 唰! 变!

Abracadabra!

Kàn! Nǐ de yīfu yě piàoliàng le.

看! 你 的 衣服 也 漂亮 了。

Look! You are also wearing a beautiful gown.

Cinderella

Nǐ de tóufa yě piàoliàng le.

你 的 头发 也 漂亮 了。

Your hair is also beautiful.

Wa!

哇！

Wa !

Chorus: *(Sung to the tune of the chorus of "Jingle Bells")*

帮 帮 忙， 帮 帮 忙， 仙 女 帮 帮 忙，

Bāng bāng máng, bāng bāng máng, xiān nǚ bāng bāng máng,

Helped me out, helped me out, Fairy Godmother helped me out,

帮 帮 忙， 帮 帮 忙， 仙 女 帮 帮 忙。

Bāng bāng máng, bāng bāng máng, xiān nǚ bāng bāng máng.

Helped me out, helped me out, Fairy Godmother helped me out.

Cinderella :

Xièxie! Xièxie! Xièxie xiānnǚ!

谢谢! 谢谢! 谢谢仙女!

Thank you, thank you! Many thanks, Fairy Godmother!

Fairy Godmother:

Huīgūniáng!

灰 姑 娘，

Cinderella,

灰姑娘

Jìzhù shíèr diǎn huíjiā.

记住 十二 点 回家。

Remember that you must return home at midnight.

Yào jìzhù! Yào jìzhù!

要 记住! 要 记住!

Remember! Remember!

Cinderella:

Jìzhù le! Jìzhù le!

记住 了! 记住 了!

I'll remember! I'll remember!

Zàijiàn! Zàijiàn!

再 见! 再 见!

Good-bye! Good-bye!

Scene 4

Narrator:

Wángzǐ àishàng le Huīgūniáng.

王子 爱上 了 灰姑娘.

As soon as the prince saw Cinderella, he fell in love with her.

Prince:

Gūniáng, nǐ jiào shénme míngzi?

姑娘, 你 叫 什么 名字?

Maiden, what is your name?

Cinderella

Chorus: *(Sing:* 你叫什么名字? Nǐ jiào shénme míngzi?*)*

你　叫　什么名字?　什么名字?　什么名字?

Nǐ　jiào　shěn me míng zi?　Shén me míng zi?　shén me mǐng zi?

What is your name? Your name? Your name?

你　　叫　什么　名字?　我　叫　灰姑娘。

Nǐ　　jiào　shén me míng zi?　Wǒ　jiào　Huīgūniáng.

What is your name? My name is Cinderella.

Prince :

Qǐng gēn wǒ tiàowǔ ba.

请 跟 我 跳舞 吧。

May I have this dance?

Narrator :

Huīgūniáng gāoxìng de qù tiàowǔ.

灰姑娘 高兴 地 去 跳舞。

Cinderella happily danced with the prince.

Tāmén tiào de hěn hǎo, hěn měi.

他们 跳得 很 好，很 美。

She and the prince danced beautifully.

灰姑娘

Scene 5

Narrator:

Hūrán jiān, zhōng xiǎng le.

忽然 间，钟 响 了。

Suddenly, the clock struck.

Dāng, dāng, dāng! Shí'èr diǎn le!

当，当，当! 十二点 了!

Dang, dang, dang! Midnight!

Chorus: *(Sung to the tune of "Michael Finnegan")*

一 点，两 点，三 点 钟。 四 点，五 点，六 点 钟。

Yí diǎn, liǎng diǎn, sān diǎn zhōng. Sì diǎn, wǔ diǎn, liù diǎn zhōng.

One o'clock, two o'clock, three o'clock. Four o'clock, five o'clock, six o'clock.

七 点，八 点，九 点 钟。 十，十一，十 二 点 钟。

Qī diǎn, bā diǎn, jiǔ diǎn zhōng. Shí, shí yī, shí èr diǎn zhōng.

Seven o'clock, eight o'clock, nine o'clock. Ten, eleven, twelve o'clock.

Cinderella:

Duìbuqǐ! Wǒ yào huíjiā le!

对不起! 我 要 回家 了!

I am sorry! I must go home!

Narrator :

Tūrán, tā diū le yìzhī xié.

突然，她 丢 了 一只 鞋。

Suddenly, Cinderella lost one of her shoes.

Cinderella

Chorus: *(Sung to the tune of "Frère Jacques")*

灰　姑　娘，　灰　姑　娘！跑　得　快，
Huī　gū niáng,　Huī　gū niáng! Pǎo de kuài,
Cinderella, Cinderella! Run fast,

跑　得　快，一　只　鞋　丢　了，一　只　鞋　丢　了。
Pǎo de kuài, Yì zhī xié diū le, yì zhī xié diū le.
Run fast! She lost one shoe, she lost one shoe.

真　可　惜，　真　可　惜！
Zhēn kě xī,　Zhēn kě xī!
What a shame, what a shame!

Scene 6

Prince and King's Messenger:
Zhè shì shéi de xié ? Shéi de xié?
这 是 谁 的 鞋? 谁 的 鞋?
Whose shoe is this ? Whose is it?

Stepsisters 1 and 2:
Shì wǒ de! Shì wǒ de!
是 我 的! 是 我 的!
It's mine! It's mine!

King's Messenger:
Búshi, nǐ de jiǎo tài dà le!
不 是, 你 的 脚 太 大 了!
No, your feet are too big!

灰姑娘

Cinderella:
Shì wǒ de.
是 我 的。
It's mine.

Prince:
Shì ma? Shì nǐ de ma?
是 吗? 是 你 的 吗?
Is it? Is it yours?

Cinderella:
Shì, wángzǐ.
是, 王 子。
Yes, my prince.

Chorus: *(Sung to the tune of the chorus of "Jingle Bells")*

谁 谁 谁 谁 谁 谁, 鞋 子 是 谁 的?
Shéi shéi shéi, shéi shéi shéi, xié zi shì shéi de?
Who who who, who who who, whose shoe is it?

谁 谁 谁 谁 谁 谁? 属 于 灰 姑 娘。
Shéi shéi shéi, shéi shéi shéi? Shǔ yú Huī gū niáng.
Who who who, who who who? It is Cinderella's.

Prince:
Wǒ hěn ài nǐ. Qǐng nǐ jià gěi wǒ ba,
我 很 爱 你。 请 你 嫁 给 我 吧,
I love you so much. Please marry me,

yìshēng péibàn wǒ.
一 生 陪 伴 我。
and be with me forever.

Cinderella

Narrator:

Cóngcǐ yǐhòu,

从此 以后，

From that time forward,

Huīgūniáng hé wángzǐ kuàilè de shēnghuó zài yìqǐ.

灰姑娘 和 王子 快乐 地 生活 在 一起。

Cinderella and the prince lived happily ever after.

Chorus: *(Sung to the tune of* "老师早呀" "Lǎoshī Zǎo Ya")

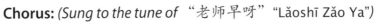

祝 你 快 乐! 祝 你 们 快 乐!
Zhù nǐ kuài lè! Zhù nǐ men kuài lè!

We wish you happiness! We wish you happiness!

我 们 今 天 祝 你 们 快 乐!
Wǒ men jīn tiān zhù nǐ men kuài lè!

Today we wish you happiness!

Game Pieces

Cut out the game pieces you need. To make a game cube, fold on the dotted lines and tape the cube together.

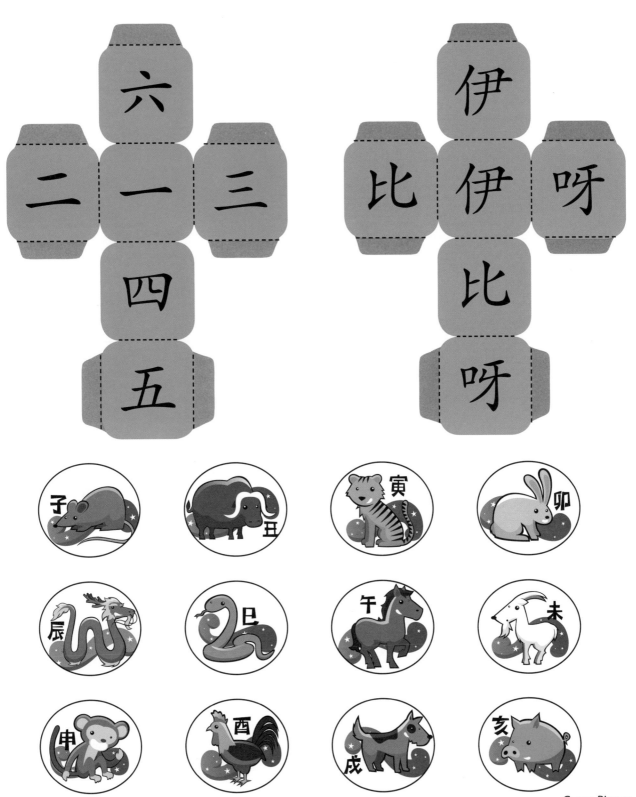

Bingo

You Might Also Like . . .

Step by Step

This colorfully illustrated collection of graded readers is designed for young Chinese language learners. All of the books in this standards-based series relate to topics integral to K–2 curricula, such as family, school, nutrition, and math. Vocabulary acquisition spirals through each topic, giving students opportunities to encounter words in multiple meaningful contexts.

Little Dragon Tales

A collection of 12 classic Chinese children's songs with a modern twist! Produced by the Emmy-winning Dave Liang of The Shanghai Restoration Project, this energetic audio CD features the young talent of Yip's Children's Choir Canada. English and Chinese lyrics with *pinyin* are included with the Audio CD.

Watch them perform at **www.littledragontales.com**.

Songs include:
Where Is Spring? (春天在哪里? Chūntiān zài nǎlǐ?)
Congratulations (恭喜恭喜 Gōngxǐ gōngxǐ)
Feng Yang Flower Drum (凤阳花鼓 Fèng Yáng huāgǔ)
Little White Boat (小白船 Xiǎo bái chuán)

Setting the Stage for Chinese

This innovative two-volume compilation of bilingual plays introduces students to Chinese language and culture as they read each story and perform their roles on stage. Topics include China's favorite stories and fairytales, along with popular Western fables. Plays are in simplified Chinese characters, *pinyin,* and English.

Visit **www.cheng-tsui.com** to view samples, place orders, and browse other language-learning materials.